Contents

RUSTLE!

DONOVAN BIXLEY'S
NATIVE PLANTS OF AOTEAROA

A catalogue record for this book is available
from the National Library of New Zealand.

ISBN 978-1-86971-457-4

A Little Moa Book

Published in New Zealand in 2023
by Hachette Aotearoa New Zealand
(an imprint of Hachette New Zealand Limited)
Level 2, 23 O'Connell Street, Auckland, New Zealand
www.hachette.co.nz

Cover and internal design by Donovan Bixley
Printed by Toppan Leefung Printing Limited, China

Warning!
Don't pick or
eat any plants
when you are in
the bush.

LITTLE
MOA

Ponga SILVER FERN

You can't miss the sight of a silver fern when walking in the New Zealand bush. The underside of its huge fronds are bright white, unlike any other fern in the forest. Ponga are found only in New Zealand, making them a unique symbol of Aotearoa.

The koru, or unfurling frond of the ponga, is an image used across Aotearoa and in traditional Māori art to represent life and growth.

The Silver fern was first used as a symbol by New Zealand rugby teams touring overseas.

Today it's like a second New Zealand flag, and is recognised all over the world.

Ponga fronds can be 4 metres long!

When hunting in the bush at night, Māori would lay silver fern fronds on the ground, underside up, to mark their pathway home.

The word 'punga' is an English mispronunciation of ponga. Punga is often used to describe all types of our native tree ferns.

SIZE

WHERE PONGA NATURALLY GROW

3

Kauri

A fully grown kauri is unmistakable with its thick, smooth-sided trunk. Kauri are not our tallest tree, but their fat trunks make them our most massive. The largest and oldest kauri is Tāne Mahuta, 'God of the Forest'. It measures 15.44 metres around the trunk and is still growing.

Kauri have no fruit or flowers to attract birds. They rely on the wind to spread their seeds.

Kauri grow naturally only in the upper North Island, but they have been planted in cooler parts of the country.

TĀNE MAHUTA
2000 YEARS
OLD

200
YEARS
OLD

SIZE

Kauri trees have existed since dinosaurs roamed the planet. Imagine ... there used to be kauri even larger than Tāne Mahuta!

Tāne
Mahuta

● WHERE KAURI
NATURALLY GROW

4

Older kauri have bark that flakes off in patches. This stops other plants clinging to the trunk.

When kauri branches break off, large amounts of gum drip from the wound. Over thousands of years this gum collects in huge deposits beneath the tree.

Kauri gum has a fragrant aroma, and was used for torches, fire starters, and even chewing gum!

Pōhutukawa

Look at that tree clinging perilously to the sea cliffs. Pōhutukawa are one of the few trees that thrive in sea spray. Older pōhutukawa often have twisted branches swooping down to the sea. They can even live with their branches and roots soaking in the high-tide water.

Pōhutukawa seeds can survive being frozen or spending a month in salt water. These tough seeds take root even on barren lava flows, like Rangitoto Island. No wonder they dominate our coastal cliffs.

I need to shave!

SIZE

Some pōhutukawa have 'aerial roots', which hang from branches like a long beard. When trees sprout from cliffs, these thread-like roots grip tight in tiny cracks.

The pōhutukawa is an iconic image of summer in northern New Zealand. Brilliant red flowers brighten up the tree like festive decorations in the weeks leading up to Christmas.

Pōhutukawa are New Zealand's Christmas tree.

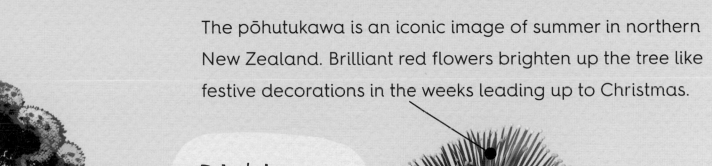

Before humans arrived in Aotearoa, pōhutukawa grew only in the north of the North Island. The colourful trees have since been planted in more southern parts of the country.

● WHERE PŌHUTUKAWA NATURALLY GROW

Kōwhai

What is that tree weighed down with little flowers drooping like bells? The bright yellow kōwhai flower is a beloved emblem of Aotearoa — you might even find one in your own backyard!

Kōwhai seeds can survive for years in the water and trees are often found growing near lakes and rivers. These waterways help spread seeds far.

In te reo Māori kōwhai means yellow. Māori planted the colourful trees around Aotearoa as they settled in new parts of the country.

● WHERE KŌWHAI ARE FOUND

In Spring, tūī are a common sight dangling like acrobats to get sweet nectar from kōwhai flowers. Kērerū also love kōwhai, stripping the trees and scoffing the leaves and flowers whole.

MUNCH MUNCH

Unlike most native New Zealand trees, some kōwhai are deciduous.

Deciduous trees lose their leaves in the winter. BRRRRR!

SIZE

Rimu

Did you see that tree draped with long branchlets of weeping green leaves? Rimu has dark reddish bark, with a distinctive pattern that looks like ridges on a map.

Captain Cook made the first beer to be brewed in New Zealand from twigs and leaves of rimu when he visited Aotearoa in 1773.

My crew said it tastes like champagne.

I've never tasted champagne.

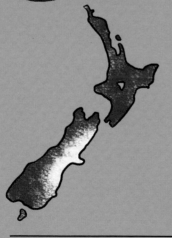

WHERE RIMU
NATURALLY GROW

Every three to four years, rimu produce huge amounts of fruit, which is known as a mast seeding.

We kākāpō are one of the most endangered birds in the world.

The survival of New Zealand's flightless kākāpō parrots depends on rimu mast seeding. The bumper crop of berries is essential to raise healthy chicks.

Rimu fruit are rich in calcium - perfect for growing bones. Baby kākāpō can eat 6000 every night!

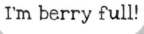

I'm berry full!

SIZE

Kahikatea

Kahikatea are our tallest native tree. Young trees have a distinctive cone-shaped top. As they get older, the tall straight trunk becomes more visible and has a crown of leaves that can look scraggly and lopsided. Kahikatea can live for over 600 years.

Not many trees can survive in waterlogged swamps like kahikatea can. Before Europeans arrived, huge forests of these giant trees grew throughout the Waikato and Hauraki wetlands.

Early European settlers cut down kahikatea thinking it would be perfect for tall ship masts and boat building. Little did they know, this water-loving tree rots quickly once it is cut down.

NZ's tallest kahikatea

● WHERE KAHIKATEA NATURALLY GROW

When in season, kahikatea fruit was a favourite food for traditional Māori feasts but only the bravest climbers could collect berries from Aotearoa's tallest treetops.

WORLD'S TALLEST TREE, USA
COAST REDWOOD
116.07 M

MOUNTAIN ASH
81.21 M

KAHIKATEA
66.5 M

The tallest kahikatea is 66.5 metres high! However, the tallest tree in New Zealand is an exotic Australian Mountain Ash.

Exotic means that this tree comes from overseas. Like us possums, Mountain Ash are not native to Aotearoa.

SIZE COMPARISON

13

Tī Kōuka CABBAGE TREE

Did you see that tree with the spiky head on a thin wobbly trunk? Tī kōuka can be seen right across Aotearoa in clusters among swampy areas, or sometimes as a single huge tree all alone.

The tap root of the tī kōuka looks like a long white carrot and is filled with natural sugars. Māori cooked the root and saved it for long journeys, where travellers could chew it like sugar cane.

Sweet as bro!

Tī kōuka leaves are especially durable in water. Māori traditionally used them to weave rain capes, nets, sandals and anchor ropes.

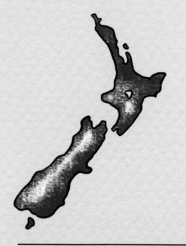

● WHERE TĪ KŌUKA NATURALLY GROW

SIZE

These holes in the cabbage tree leaves are munched by the Cabbage Tree caterpillar. After its metamorphosis, the adult moth is a master of disguise — perfectly camouflaged among the patterns of the dry leaves hanging down.

Tī kōuka have the incredible power to regenerate. Even if the tree is cut to the ground it will continue to grow and come back from the dead.

Most fully grown cabbage trees have hollow trunks and store water in the wood. This makes the wood so fire-resistant that early European settlers used the tī kōuka as chimneys on their huts.

Pūriri

Have you come across a gnarled old tree in the forest? If it was covered in bright pink flowers, you may have stumbled upon an ancient pūriri.

Taketakerau, NZ's oldest pūriri

● WHERE PŪRIRI NATURALLY GROW

Even when knocked down or split apart the pūriri continues to grow, forming huge twisted trunks. The wood is also fire-resistant. No wonder they are one of our oldest living trees and can grow to be over 2000 years old!

Pūriri moth grubs leave scars on trees from burrowing into the trunks where they live. After six years the pūriri grub emerges from its burrow as a beautiful green moth.

Most plants bloom only once a year, but pūriri have flowers and fruit all year round, making them an important food source for many of our native birds and insects.

I'm New Zealand's largest moth, but I only live for a few days.

SIZE

Pūriri wood is so tough it can blunt an axe. It was used by Māori to make tools for splitting other softer wood.

Tōtara

Ouch! Careful of that tree — it has spiky leaves. The trunk of the tōtara has long strips of flaky bark, and this mighty tree can live for more than 1500 years. Unlike the long-lived kauri and pūriri, the hardy tōtara conquer every landscape of Aotearoa — from hot to cold, north to south, high to low — making tōtara a true rangatira, a great chief of New Zealand plants.

Throughout Polynesia, tōtara shares its name with the porcupine fish for good reason: each tōtara branch is covered in thousands of spiky leaves, keeping them safe from munching animals.

Pouakani, NZ's oldest tōtara

● WHERE TŌTARA NATURALLY GROW

SIZE

Endangered native bats, like me, need native forest with old trees to live in. The hollow trunks of ancient tōtara make the perfect home for us to roost during the day or in cold weather.

Tōtara wood is resistant to bugs and rot, even when logs have been in the water for years. Tōtara wood is 25 per cent lighter than kauri wood, making it the favourite wood of Māori for carving a grand waka.

Horoeka LANCEWOOD

Have you seen a plant that looks like an arrow pointing up to the sky? Young horoeka have distinctive leathery leaves that are up to one metre long. They can stay in this form for more than fifteen years before growing into the adult tree — which has a trunk that looks like old twisted rope and a rounded top of short green leaves.

Horoeka is one of the most unusual trees in the world. The young tree and the adult tree look so different that they were once thought to be two different types of plant.

EEEK!
Māori once used the long straight trunks to make bird-hunting tao (lances), which gives the tree its English name, lancewood.

SIZE

No one knows why horoeka have such different stages of growth. Some believe the tree may have developed tough spiky leaves over thousands of years to protect the young plants from being eaten by giant moa. Once fully grown, the leaves of the adult horoeka would have then been beyond the reach of these now extinct giant birds.

I wish I could reach those tasty leaves!

● WHERE HOROEKA NATURALLY GROW

Nīkau

Nīkau palms are found only in New Zealand. With their tall, skinny trunk and fan shaped crown of leaves, they add a tropical feel to our landscape in warmer parts of the country where they grow.

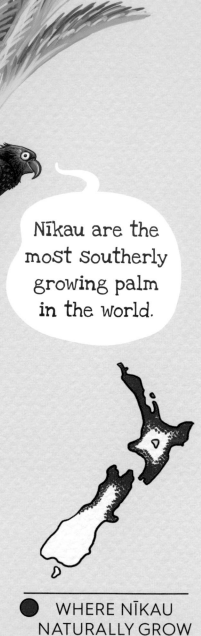

Nīkau are the most southerly growing palm in the world.

Nīkau grow painfully slowly, taking 40 years to establish in the soil before growing a trunk. Adult trees can take 200 years to reach 10 metres tall.

● WHERE NĪKAU NATURALLY GROW

If you see a flowering nīkau it is at least 70 years old.

SIZE

Nīkau flowers are an important food source, first attracting insects. As larger flowers open, tauhou (silvereyes), korimako (bellbirds) and tūī drink the nectar. Then kererū and kaka feast on the ripe red fruit, spreading the seeds widely.

The ripe nīkau berries are too hard to be eaten by humans. Māori used them to make necklaces instead.

Tawhai SOUTHERN BEECHES

Over half of Aotearoa's native forest is made up of beech trees, including: tawhairaunui (red and hard beech), and tawhairauriki (black and mountain beech).

Beech forests are some of our prettiest park-like native areas. Small beech leaves carpet the ground and dappled light filters through the branches giving the forest an airy feel.

Unlike beech trees in other parts of the world, New Zealand beech trees are unique in that they are evergreen.

● WHERE SOUTHERN BEECH FORESTS NATURALLY GROW

Evergreen trees keep their leaves all year round. So cosy in winter.

In summer, the beech forest gives off a lovely fragrance. This is caused by tiny scale insects that burrow into the bark and feed off the beech tree's sugary sap. The insects excrete excess sugars as honeydew.

I eat sugar and I poop sugar.

Microscopic fungi grow within the honeydew. The fungi can cover the trunk in a velvety black coating.

Many animals feast on the honeydew including tūī, kākā, bees, and lizards.

Watch out! Exotic wasps also love to collect honeydew from beech trees. They can be dangerous in summer.

SIZE

Mānuka

Look at that spindly bush with flaky black bark peeling off its twisted trunk. In spring, mānuka are covered with beautiful flowers of white or deep crimson.

Mānuka leaves and bark contain oils that are antibacterial, anti-fungal and antiviral. Māori used mānuka to relieve fevers and stomach aches. Early European sailors and settlers made tea from mānuka and referred to them as tea trees.

ARRRRRRR!

Sorry, I mean, Ahhhh! That tastes good!

SIZE

Mānuka pollen makes a strong dark honey, which is sought after all over the world.

Mānuka's black bark is caused by a sooty mould, like that which can grow on beech trees.

Oils found in mānuka bark help fire to burn more ferociously. Mānuka seeds pop open when exposed to flames and grow well afterwards. Centuries ago, when Māori and pākehā used fire to clear forest, it resulted in mānuka taking over massive areas of newly cleared land. Now mānuka is found all across Aotearoa.

● WHERE MĀNUKA NATURALLY GROW

Harakeke

Did you see those plants with long, pointed leaves fanning out from the ground? Harakeke can be found all over Aotearoa, especially in swampy areas and beside rivers. For traditional Māori it was the most important plant in the land. Every pā had its own harakeke plantation.

Harakeke flowers are important for nectar feeders like me.

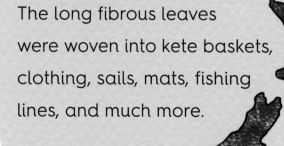

In the legend of How Māui Slowed the Sun, Māui teaches us how to weave harakeke into three different types of rope.

The long fibrous leaves were woven into kete baskets, clothing, sails, mats, fishing lines, and much more.

SIZE

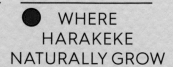

● WHERE HARAKEKE NATURALLY GROW

Toetoe

Check out that tall stem with a top like blonde hair waving in the wind. Toetoe is a common sight across Aotearoa, from the coast to the mountains. But be careful when passing toetoe! The leaves have sharp edges that can cut into skin. The flower stems were used by Māori for lining the inner walls of whare.

Not to be confused with exotic pampas grass, which is a pest plant in Aotearoa and looks more like candy floss on a stick. Eww!

Hollow toetoe stems were also perfect for straws, and lightweight frames for kites – manu tukutuku.

SIZE

● WHERE TOETOE NATURALLY GROW

Horopito

Have you come across a bush with red splotchy leaves? Horopito leaves are spicy and hot to chew. Today horopito is used as a flavouring in modern restaurants and Māori kai.

Traditional Māori used horopito as rongoā, a medicinal plant for all sorts of illnesses including toothache. Early Europeans called it 'Māori painkiller'.

YUCK! Too spicy for us!

URRGH! Horopito protects itself against pests like me.

Our plants are a natural taonga, a treasure, found only in Aotearoa. With care we can keep our native forests thriving.

SIZE

WHERE HOROPITO NATURALLY GROW

Which New Zealand
plant is your
favourite?